AF488397

little
birdie
babies

Written and illustrated by
Heather Boschke

Little Birdie Babies

ISBN 979-8-9869794-2-7
Library of Congress Control Number 2024904186

Written and illustrated by Heather Boschke | Buddha Birdie
Layout and design by Paul Nylander | Illustrada

Buddha Birdie LLC
Burnsville, Minnesota

buddhabirdie.com

Dedication

To my mama bird.

Thank you for helping me stand tall
and believing I could fly before
I even had wings.

What do you know about baby birds?

When birds are ready to have babies, they build nests. Just like people have different kinds of houses, birds have different types of nests.

Some birds stack leaves, grasses, mosses, sticks, and even feathers together to create a little house.

Other birds make a small bowl out of grass and twigs and mud.

Some birds nest on the ground, and some nest high up in tall trees.

Each bird makes a home that's just right for them.

Every baby bird comes from an egg.

Mama birds lay eggs in the nest they have built. Baby birds grow inside their eggs until they're ready to come out.

When a bird is born, it's called hatching. This is when the bird breaks out of its egg.

Birds grow up really fast!

In just a few weeks, they go from tiny
babies with no feathers to young
adults who are big enough to fly.

When baby birds are first born, they
are called hatchlings. Baby birds that still live
in the nest are called nestlings. And young birds that have
grown enough feathers to begin trying to fly are called
fledglings.

Let's learn more about baby birds and how their
adventures start!

walker is a baby house wren.

Baby house wrens are called chicks. House wrens build their nests in many different places. They nest in tree holes, bushes, woodpiles, and even hanging planters! House wrens often make their nests in birdhouses.

The parents gather small twigs to create a cup-shaped space for the eggs.

"I'm ready to
leave the nest
only two weeks
after hatching!"
says Walker.

"I have lots of
brothers and sisters
and love traveling
with my family,"
says Tommy.

Tommy is a baby turkey.

A baby turkey is called a poult. Poults are born with fluffy feathers that can be yellow, brown, or gray. As poults get older, new feathers grow and they start to look more like their parents.

Turkey families can be big! A turkey mom can raise ten or more poults at once.

Poppy is a baby piping plover.

Baby piping plovers are called chicks. Piping plovers are known as shorebirds because they live on the edges of bodies of water.

Piping plovers lay eggs that are very small: the size of a dime! The eggs are a creamy tan color and speckled with brown splotches. This helps the eggs stay hidden on the beaches where they are laid in small holes.

"I don't need my parents to feed me! I can walk around and find food soon after hatching," says Poppy.

"I could swim
all by myself
when I was just
a few hours old!"
says Teddy.

Teddy is a baby trumpeter swan.

A baby swan is called a cygnet. Swans build their nests of sticks and grasses near water so cygnets can grow up close to meals of plants and small fish.

Even though trumpeter swans are named for the loud, trumpeting calls that the adults make, cygnets start with softer peeps and whistles. As they grow, their calls become louder and more trumpet-like.

Pippa is a baby emperor penguin.

Baby penguins are called chicks. Emperor penguin eggs stay warm and safe snuggled on their dads' feet, tucked under a special flap of skin called a brood pouch.

When they hatch, emperor penguin chicks are covered in thick and fluffy gray feathers. Their feathers keep them warm, which is important because they live in Antarctica, one of the coldest places on Earth!

"I don't have a nest! When I'm inside my egg, I stay warm underneath my dad," says Pippa.

Griffin is a baby great horned owl.

Baby owls are called owlets. Great horned owls do not build their own nests. Instead, they use nests left by other large birds or animals.

As owlets grow, they start branching. This means they explore outside the nest and try out their wings by jumping onto nearby branches.

Owlets also practice hissing and whistling so they are ready to make the adult call, which sounds like "Who's awake? Me too!"

"I practice
for flying by
hopping on
tree branches
and flapping
my wings,"
says Griffin.

"I chirp really
loud to let
my parents
know when
I'm hungry!"
says Ray.

Ray is a baby robin.

Baby robins are called chicks. They hatch from bright blue eggs. Robins' nests look like little bowls made from twigs and grass and mud.

Robin chicks eat a lot and grow very fast. They are the same size as their parents in just two weeks!

Georgie is a baby Canada goose.

A baby goose is called a gosling. Goslings stay with their parents for the first year of their lives, and sometimes longer.

Goslings are really good at copying what their parents do, and they learn super fast! They can swim soon after hatching, and they can fly when they are two to three months old.

"I like to play follow-the-leader
when I'm walking or
swimming with
my family,"
says Georgie.

"I come from
a tiny egg the
size of a small
jellybean!"
says Rowan.

Rowan is a baby ruby-throated hummingbird.

A baby hummingbird is called a chick. These itty-bitty birds live in a small, cup-shaped nest made from spider silk and soft plant material. These nests are often hidden under the branches and leaves of a tree.

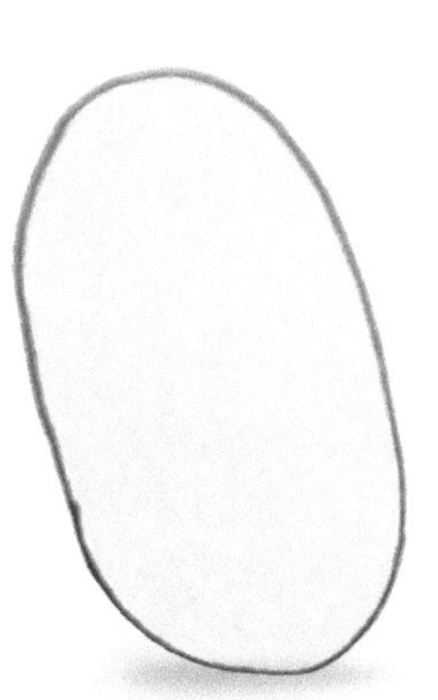

Hummingbird chicks need to eat every twenty minutes! This makes the mama bird super busy. She goes back and forth to find food and bring it to the nest.

Sully is a baby sandhill crane.

Baby sandhill cranes are called colts. They hatch in nests made from plants and mud on the ground in wetland areas.

Sandhill cranes are known for their dancing, and colts learn to dance too! They practice by jumping and flapping their wings.

"I stay
close to my
mom and
dad, and we
dance and
play together!"
says Sully.

"I can
walk and
run and
feed myself
soon after hatching!"
says Kit.

Kit is a baby killdeer.

Baby killdeer are called chicks. These shorebirds don't make typical nests. Killdeer mamas lay their eggs in shallow holes in the ground, often in rocky areas.

Killdeer parents protect their nests by pretending to have a broken wing. They use this trick to keep predators away from the nest.

Willow is a baby wood duck.

Duck babies are called ducklings. Wood ducks make nests in tree trunks, often in holes created by woodpeckers. These nests can be really high off the ground.

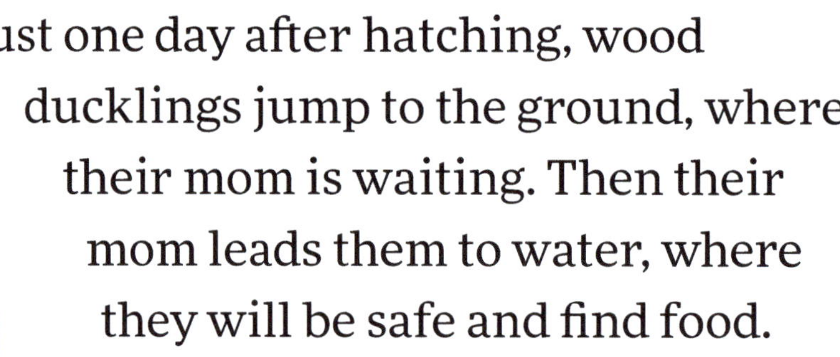

Just one day after hatching, wood ducklings jump to the ground, where their mom is waiting. Then their mom leads them to water, where they will be safe and find food.

"I made
a big jump
from my nest
all the way down
to the ground, and
I didn't get hurt at all!"
says Willow.

"I like eating fish
for breakfast,
lunch, and dinner!"
says Benji.

Benji is a baby great blue heron.

Baby great blue herons are called chicks. Great blue herons nest together in big groups called rookeries. A rookery can have more than a hundred other nests!

Great blue herons nest high in the trees near rivers, lakes, or wetlands. Being close to water is important because blue herons eat fish.

These chicks are known for their loud squawks, which sound like "Kwok! Kwok!"

Baby birds all have special beginnings.

While all baby birds start from an egg, they grow up in different ways.

Which baby bird did you like the best? What makes them special to you?

Just like these baby birds, you are growing and learning every day.

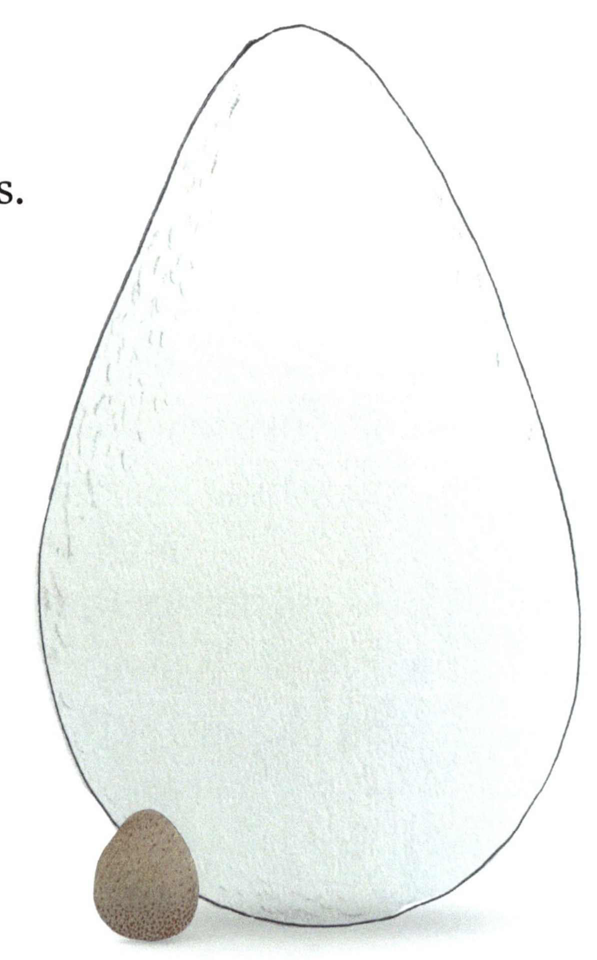

So spread your
wings, be brave,
and fly toward
your dreams.

Keeping Baby Birds Safe

Baby birds must be kept safe while they are young so they can grow up to be strong adult birds.

Baby birds are often very quiet, especially when their parents are away from the nest. This helps them hide from predators.

Bird parents
protect their eggs
and babies. They guard
their nests and chase other
animals away.

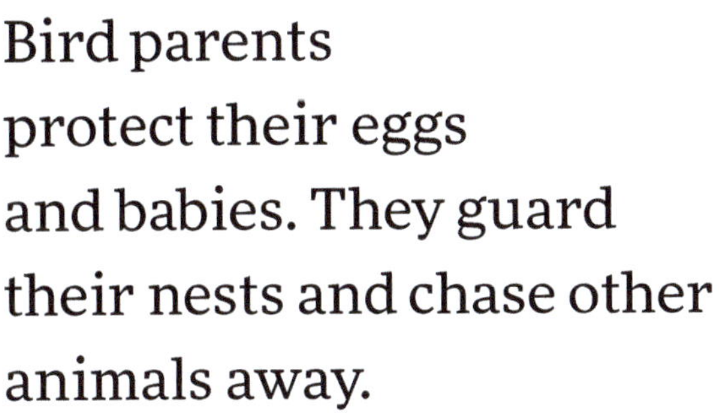

It's important to leave
baby birds alone. If you
find one that is hurt, a
wildlife center can tell you
how to help.

About the Author

Heather's nickname is "Heather Feather." One of her favorite spring memories is watching a mama hummingbird build a nest and raise babies in a tree in her backyard. Heather creates her bird drawings with pen and marker, and she always gives them names.

Contact Heather and see more of her bird drawings at www.buddhabirdie.com.

www.ingramcontent.com/pod-product-compliance
Lightning Source LLC
Chambersburg PA
CBHW042031110726
48010CB00008B/302